Journo*LISTS*

201 ways to improve your journalism

They don't come more hands-on than this! Journo*LISTS* is a treasure house of good advice for journalists and PR people. From finding news to deciding what colours to use in a page, a leading training consultant digs to the deepest level of practicality to find the answers that really make a difference.

About the author

Cedric Pulford is one of the UK's most experienced journalism trainers and a practising freelance journalist. He worked successively on four daily newspapers, including one in the United States. He has had a long association with the Guardian, as a staff subeditor and latterly as a syndication editor. His writing credits include the Guardian, Daily Telegraph, Observer Foreign News Service, Gemini News, Ecumenical News International and Thompson's (Toronto). Cedric Pulford headed the Plymouth-based editorial training scheme for Mirror Group Newspapers before becoming an independent media consultant in 1982. He has worked extensively in developing countries, particularly in Africa and Asia. For several years his company has run skills improvement courses for media people in association with the National Council for the Training of Journalists.

Journo*LISTS*

201 ways to improve your journalism

Cedric Pulford

ITURI

Copyright © 2001, Cedric Pulford
The moral rights of the author have been asserted

Published 2001 by Ituri Publications
39 Portway
Banbury, Oxon OX16 7QH (UK)

ISBN 0 9536430 1 8

Text set in 11pt on 14pt Palatino,
with headings in Arial,
by Book Production Services, London

Printed in Great Britain
by St Edmundsbury Press, Bury St Edmunds, Suffolk

A CIP catalogue record for this book is available from the Britsh
Library

Contents

For Auntie Mary

100 years old
November 8, 2000

Acknowledgements

Grateful thanks to those whose help with this book has been gladly given: author and columnist Keith Waterhouse, whose visits to Plymouth so impressed Mirror Group trainee journalists and their training manager, for writing the foreword; Paul Hopkins, former training manager of the National Council for the Training of Journalists, for fruitfully combing over the draft text and for creating the index; John Ezard, Bob Smyth and Roderick Thomson for valued advice on the material; Andrew Boyd for thinking of a title (again); Georgina Rhodes and Richard Proctor of Rhodes and Proctor for their cover design (again). Of course, I alone am responsible for any mistakes that remain.

CP

Foreword
by Keith Waterhouse

Over the years I have accumulated a whole shelf of English textbooks for journalists. Indeed, I have written one myself. But all-important though a firm grasp of the language is for anyone working in newspapers, there is far more to the job than evading hanging participles.

Apart from Harold Evans' encyclopedic work there have been few manuals, until now, concerned with the nuts and bolts of journalism. Cedric Pulford fills a gap.

He has run courses in journalism over many years, and from them have emerged some of the most eminent figures in the business – not, true enough, fully fledged, but thrown out of the nest to flitter-flutter as they may.

Cedric's 201 tips for people in the news business are nothing if not practical. No time here for theorising: it is about earning a living.

Thus we proceed briskly through the newsroom from arts reviews to writing headlines, from the dreaded advertorials (someone has to write them) to picture captions, news structure, quotes, writing features and interviews, and the rest. And yes, the hanging participle does get a look-in: see the section on language traps. On the use of English, I particularly value the caution against swallowing other people's jargon – the only authorities who can be safely quoted as gospel are Matthew, Mark, Luke and John.

While wide-ranging, this refreshingly compact manual is not comprehensive and doesn't pretend to be – even after 50 years in the business one still doesn't know all the answers, nor even some of the questions.

But I wish I had had something like this to help me along the way all those years ago. Some old hands are fond of saying that journalism can't be taught. I think that what they mean is that it can't be learned, unless the instinct for it is there. I can think of no better aid than Cedric Pulford's pithy guide.

Keith Waterhouse, CBE, FRSL, is a prolific writer of novels, plays and screenplays including *Billy Liar* (novel), *Jeffrey Bernard Is Unwell* (play) and *Whistle Down The Wind* and *A Kind of Loving* (screenplays with Willis Hall). He has been a journalist since 1950, with columns in the Daily Mirror (1970-86) and Daily Mail (since 1986). His popular *Newspaper Style* (1989) is a revised and expanded version of the stylebook he wrote for the Daily Mirror. He also wrote *English Our English* (1991), and he was a member, 1987-88, of the Kingman Committee on the Teaching of English.

Introduction

THIS book has its origin in courses about journalism that I have run for many years. Mainly the attendees are practising media people – journalists and press officers. Their professional concerns are overwhelmingly practical: how to write better articles and press releases, how to produce better headlines, how to lay out better pages and proof them effectively, how to juggle the conflicting demands of editorial and advertising. The same issues come up again and again. That's why it seems appropriate to share some of the answers we have evolved with a wider readership.

This is not yet another journalism textbook. Theory has been kept to the minimum. So too have examples, which become tedious if overdone. It is intended strictly as a "doing" book for working media people. Among the 201 tips, everyone will, I hope, find something to help them improve their professional output.

Reporters, feature writers, subeditors, press officers – we are all in the news business, and if we fail to produce news all our professional techniques are in vain. Particularly with corporate publications, for internal or external consumption, but in other areas of journalism too, material gets printed that fails the core test of news.

So the right place to begin this set of practical pointers is: **Remember the twofold test for news: newness and relevance.** If the chairman says people are the company's greatest resource, that may be an important statement but it certainly isn't a news statement when the readers have heard it a hundred times before. There is no journalistic reason for the remarks to be the front-page lead. On the other hand, the world is full of things that people don't know and don't need to know. To be news, information must impact on them at some level – in the wallet or purse, as curious human beings or as thoughtful citizens of the country and the world.

So news is a twofold thing. Simple really. I once worked with a veteran journalist in America, land of small-town newspapers, who used to say: "That town's so small folks read the paper to see if the editor got it right." He was joking. In reality, there and everywhere else, it ain't news if they know it, or if they don't know it and don't care.

1 Finding News

IT isn't hard to fill the news columns of newspapers and magazines. Finding news of the right quality is harder. Information pours in from organisations wanting publicity, agencies supply ready-to-use news, the diary kept by the news desk records coming events from meetings to fairs, conventions to charity stunts. Much of this material will be usable, but it is common to all, lacking our own twist of individuality and probably without much element of surprise. We need to build on these staple sources of news with more active news gathering.

Followups are everywhere. A survey by a national polling organisation found that editors rated information from other publications as their most important source of news, ahead even of material dug up by their own reporters. This rather surprising finding is a sign that we must keep our eyes on our competitors and other relevant publications big or small. It isn't only a case of following up their stories. News may lurk among the advertisements, where, for example, statutory notices may be the first occasion when a major construction scheme has come to light, or among the humble births, marriages and deaths. National newspapers draw heavily for news on local papers and specialised magazines. Sometimes the traffic is the other way, and a local or specialised angle will be spotted in a national story. Another source of followups is to revisit a story some months or a year later. Has it happened as predicted, planned? Did the politicians keep their promises? To keep track of stories like this, we need to keep our own news diaries, into which also go our scheduled meetings, appointments and interviews.

Visibility gets the tipoffs. Another type of active news gathering is stories we get from tipoffs. We'll get few of these if we aren't visible around our patch. The patch may be a geographical one for a local newspaper reporter or the round of meetings, conferences and conventions for the specialist reporter. Worthwhile information is much more likely to emerge face to face. People rarely phone in with tips unless they want something plugged.

Beware the scoop culture. Tipoffs are a major source of exclusives, which most publications covet. It was an editor not of the Sun but of the Times who said "The press lives by disclosures!". He said this in the 19th century, and since then the British press has become dominated by a culture of exclusives. Perhaps editors are too scoop-hungry: it isn't clear that readers are as concerned with scoops as editors are, and they become cynical when two or three papers claim the same story as an exclusive! We need to get exclusives but we need to give a solid service of everyday news too.

Contacts are our stock in trade. It is our contacts, rather than our knowledge or our journalistic abilities, that can give us an edge over competitors. It pays to cultivate contacts. Getting in touch now and again, not just when we are pursuing a story, helps to keep the relationship warm (and may uncover a story). Sending a cutting (clipping) of an article to someone whom we have interviewed for it is a courtesy that takes little time and is much appreciated [see chapter Interviewing].

Keep a careful contacts book. Whether we use the traditional alphabeticalised pocket book or an electronic organiser, it pays to spend a little time each week keeping our list of contacts up to date. Data in the organiser should be backed up in a PC: any electronic equipment can crash! The organiser has a great advantage over the book – as well as providing contact details for a person, it can be searched by subjects. We may want to know all the names for a particular subject. The drawback of a book is that it can be arranged by people or by subjects, but not easily by both.

Get mobile, home and direct line numbers. With those high up the pecking order, these are far more useful than the office switchboard number. Daytime calls to the office run head-on into the meeting culture. Senior executives are hardly ever at their desks and free to take calls. After an interview is often the time to get those valuable mobile, home and direct line numbers [see chapter Interviewing].

Keep a careful cuttings book. These days that can mean a folder in the PC as well as paper. To keep a cuttings book and folder isn't just vanity or even professional pride. Cuttings are our professional credits: we may be asked to show them to get our next job, or commission if we are freelance. A cuttings book can be the quickest way of remembering what we have written about a subject before and a valuable source of background information for the present story. But be aware that there may have been mistakes in the earlier stories – and allow for the passage of time in people's situations!

Know how to use the internet. Background – past facts that are relevant to the present situation – is crucial for journalism at the highest level. The internet has transformed the possibilities here. Searchable databases mean we can quickly call up reports of earlier stages of the story, comparing various newspapers' versions to help ensure that our background information is correct. Search engines may produce tasty morsels of information from somewhere in the world's archives that no cuttings library or reference books would ever manage.

Don't pay for information. Newspapers and magazines loath paying even the smallest amounts, in cash or kind, to news sources. They know that if the practice of charging for news information became general it would destroy the basis of journalism. It is more than the cost of it; paying for information encourages sources to "talk up" the facts to make them more valuable. Buy-ups, where a celebrity or someone in the news sells his or her story, are a fact of life, however. Some of this chequebook journalism sails close to the ethical wind, but buy-ups as such are not wrong. They are a world away from the idea of paying eyewitnesses for their experiences or business people and officials for interviews. In investigative journalism a payment for information may occasionally be made as the only way to crack the story. Such payments have to be strictly approved by the editor.

Don't accept gifts from news sources. Anything more than a ballpoint pen with the organisation's name on it should be politely refused or left behind. Gifts create a climate of goodwill (that's why shareholders' or taxpayers' money is spent on them), and we kid ourselves if we say that gifts don't affect our objectivity of approach to an organisation. Gifts are often not thrust into our hands but come in press packs. At a major intergovernmental conference several thousand reporters found mini-taperecorders in their press packs. We can discreetly pocket such items. We can just as discreetly leave them behind.

2 Interviewing

INTERVIEWING is the chief tool of active journalism. Without talking to people who can give us information or opinions, by phone or face to face, we can only print what others send us or recycle what has appeared somewhere else.

The more we know, the more we get. Preparation about the subject and perhaps the person to be interviewed is likely to pay rich dividends. The internet has vastly increased the possibilities for research. Time wasted in an interview establishing basic information that can be got elsewhere is time lost to new areas of questioning. A phone interview typically lasts up to 20 minutes, a face-to-face interview rather more. In-depth interviews for a celebrity profile might be scheduled for an hour, but we can't expect that length of time routinely. Thorough background knowledge will also increase interviewees' confidence in us and make them more willing to be candid.

Identify oneself as a journalist. Almost always, it isn't ethical to collect information for publication, especially the names of our interviewees, without identifying ourselves as journalists. Undercover investigation journalism is the – rare – exception, but this still has to meet clearcut criteria in the code of conduct of the Press Complaints Commission, the newspaper industry's standards body. In a phone interview or a face-to-face meeting we naturally begin by introducing ourselves and saying where we're from. When talking to members of the public it isn't sensible to go storming up notebook and tape recorder in hand. That could frighten them into silence. But somewhere along the line we have to identify ourselves. The interviewee may refuse to give his or her name, although they are unlikely to object to the information being used non-attributably [see below]. If they do, the whole interview cannot be used.

Don't ask permission to quote. We are under obligation to identify ourselves but we are under no obligation to ask interviewees' permission to quote them. To ask "Can I quote you?" invites them to wonder what they've said and to tell us no! Once an encounter has been established as a journalistic interview it's up to the source to put it, or parts of it, off the record, not up to us to put it on the record. The convention is well understood by those dealing regularly with the media, but in the name of common sense and fairness we may need to hold back some of what we have learnt from questioning members of the public. There is a category of information that can be useful: non-attributable. On the record is fully usable and fully sourceable; non-attributable is usable but not sourceable (nothing is given to identify the speaker beyond a broad group to which he or she belongs: "a neighbour", "an employee at the factory"). Off the record information is for background understanding only, and cannot be used. Informants who don't want their names used may be happy for the material to appear non-attributably.

Have a list of 'must know' questions. Whatever else comes up, we must not end the call or leave the room without the answers to these crucial questions. As well as the earth-shakers, basic things like a person's job title or the spelling of his or her name are easily overlooked. Include these among the 'must know' questions.

Start with an omnibus question. It usually saves time by asking an interviewee to begin by telling us what the thing is all about. It establishes the parameters of the subject more quickly than a string of specific questions. Having started someone going, resist the temptation to interrupt. Ask follow-up questions at the end of the outline explanation. Generally interview questions go from soft to hard, to give informants the chance to warm up and to feel comfortable with us.

Don't be afraid to ask direct questions. Questions about someone's private life or business affairs that might be rude in a social setting aren't rude in a journalistic interview. It's very unlikely that offence will be taken. If it is we have the easy, and true, answer that we're doing our job.

Ask for examples and illustrations. "The best", "the worst", "the biggest", "the toughest"? Journalism thrives on specifics, which lift otherwise dry and flat material.

Take notes as well as recordings. The only way to get a speaker's words 100% accurate is to record them. Few people's shorthand is fast enough to capture more than a few bursts of speech, and many journalists don't have shorthand at all. It is, however, worth taking the trouble to learn shorthand, with 100 words per minute as a realistic goal. Recordings take much time and effort to transcribe into usable form. We can cut this time down by using notebook and recorder simultaneously. Our notes keep track of the sequence of the conversation, and that allows us to quickly find the bit we want in the recording for the direct quotes. For the sake of speed many interviews are done with notes only. Direct quotes are reconstructed from words and phrases captured in the notebook, sometimes in longhand.

Avoid showing material before publication. Interviewees are often worried about factual accuracy, but showing material in advance of publication tends to throw the baby out with the bathwater. If we show sources an article so they can check accuracy, they would be superhuman not to object to unfavourable interpretation or comments, or even emphases, that we quite properly have made. Messy arguments are avoided if we don't show the material. We can satisfy accuracy concerns by recapping key facts and figures at the end of the interview – actually, a factual recap is no bad idea even if we aren't pushed to do it. Another way of quietening an anxious interviewee is to phone back when the article has been written, and read over the directly quoted parts. The rest of the article, including any interpretations and comments, stays private until publication! But people used to dealing with the media rarely ask to see stories in advance.

Find out a follow-up contact number. Find out where the interviewee can be reached within the next 48 hours or for whatever period the article is to be worked on, in case additional information is needed. We can't assume the person will be in the office or at home conveniently waiting for us to ring. A request for follow-up contact numbers is hard for an interviewee to refuse. It may have the useful side-effect of giving us direct line, home and mobile phone numbers of the big cheeses.

3 News Story Structure

THE difference between news and features is at the heart of journalism. Many pieces fall somewhere in between – the human interest story, for example, may use colourful feature techniques, or a news report stressing background may be so interpretative as to amount to a news feature – but most don't. They are recognisably either a news report or a feature article, and each type is structured in a distinct way. Lord Northcliffe, the creator of the (London) Daily Mail, said in a remark that remains as true as ever: "Hard news catches readers, features hold them."

Make the intro (lead) the main, specific point in the story. In news terms, the intro, or lead, is the first paragraph of the story. A good way to clear our thoughts of the welter of detail and to discover the best point to start with is to imagine we're bursting to tell a friend what happened. "Hey, have you heard…." What follows will probably make the best intro. General intros, which aim to set the scene or indicate the significance of the event, are usually not wanted. Nor are teaser intros, which belong to features. Get on with it, and tell the readers what actually happened!

Don't overload the intro with detail. The length of the all important first paragraph naturally varies from publication to publication but the usual range is between 20 and 40 words. If we are tempted to write more than 40 words in even the heaviest publications, we ought to think again. We are either putting in too much detail at this point in the story, or combining two separate aspects of the story in the opening par. One of those points belongs in the second par.

Give information in descending order of news value. While at first sight this may seem obvious, it is amazing how many stories get trapped in the chronological order of the material being covered. Points of interest in a company report or a speech, for instance, will come from anywhere, and their news value will have little connection with the order in which they are presented in the original. A disaster story will begin near the end of the chain of events – i.e. the crash itself – and is likely to go next to the condition of the injured rather than the beginning of the journey: in terms of time, that is 2 – 3 – 1.

We should repeat ourselves. In long stories, the idea of main points in descending order of importance can be done twice over – in the introductory paragraphs and again in the later pars, which are the body of the story. Separating outline and detail in this way is a good way of telling the story cleanly and without confusion. Don't be afraid of repeating points so long as the second mention adds detail. In fact, a point that is mentioned in the intro and never reappears is unsatisfactory because it leaves the reader wanting more.

Include the 'why' or 'how' high up. The six news elements are: who, what, where, when, why and how. Traditionally, these had all to be included at the very top of a story. Most people now see that as too formulaic, leading to stiff intros, but the news elements still need to be got in quickly. Who, what, where and when describe the event; why and how explain it. Why something happened or how something will be managed are among the first questions readers ask so we ought not to bury these elements amid our concern to describe the event.

Quote early and quote often. Direct quotes, the passages within speech marks, are where we tell the reader: "This is what the person actually said." Quotes are the soundbites of print. Just as a TV and radio newsreader's presentation is enlivened with the sight or sound of the event, so direct quotes add life to summarised accounts. The first quote needs to come early in the story. Lots in quotes is helpful, but having several pars in a row as quotes from the same person is, paradoxically, slowing. In an extended story we do better to have a mixture of quotes and non-quotes (including paraphrases of the speaker's words).

Pick quotes for impact. Any statement that would look just as well in paraphrased form, like "I had my breakfast at seven o'clock this morning", is not suitable for direct quotes. We are looking for statements that are either very colourful or very important, where the reader has added value from knowing the precise words used. Quotes are a very weak area in press releases and house newspapers, usually through no fault of the journalists concerned, because the person being quoted insists on stating the obvious, drowning us in jargon or entangling us in officialese or business-speak.

Keep opinions to ourselves. As an experiment, a group of practising media people listened to a politically sensitive news story read out as it appeared in the Daily Telegraph and the Guardian, two London papers with very clear political positions. The participants were unable to say which papers ran which stories, some ascribing the Telegraph story to the Guardian and others vice versa. That was an impressive illustration of the "objectivity criterion" in practice. After all, our purpose in writing news stories is to tell people what happened. It's not to tell them what we think about what happened.

Interpretation is not the same as comment. To call a decision "silly" is clearly an opinion and is out of place in a news report (unless of course a source is saying it, when his or her opinion becomes our news fact); to call that decision "controversial" or "bitterly contested" may well be an interpretation that is legitimately included in the story. Interpretation, properly used, helps the reader to understand the story more fully. Of course, we should not slip our opinion into the story in the guise of interpretation – calling an action controversial because we dislike it rather than because opinion is genuinely divided on the issue. A good test is whether all sides would agree with the descriptive words we plan to use. If they would, it's probably interpretation; if they wouldn't it's probably opinion. Everyone, for instance, would agree that the euro is "controversial" with "strongly held" views on both sides.

Background adds value. Background is information that is not part of the immediate event but which adds understanding to the story. A good neighbour scheme's 85 per cent success rate in other London boroughs is background for a report about such a scheme being introduced in our borough – but critical for the story. If it has been that successful elsewhere, it's set to be successful here also. Background is also used in another way. There's always somebody who has missed previous instalments of a running news story. One or two sentences of background recap will usually serve to make each issue's story complete in itself, and all will be able to follow it. This idea of self-containment is even more important where publication intervals are greater. More and more people will have forgotten the earlier stages of the story.

4 Writing Effective Features

THERE is nothing new in the recognition that a newspaper needs both news and features to succeed and to continue succeeding. The same is true with magazines, with the emphasis reversed: a newspaper, even today, is primarily about news, a magazine is primarily about features. The term "feature" covers the vast range of journalistic material that is not chiefly concerned to describe what happened (the news report): news features add further dimensions of understanding to straight reportage, or take a hot topic and examine it; opinion features and personal columns get us thinking; editorials, also called leading articles or leaders, suggest what we should think; arts reviews tell us what the writer thought partly as a guide to whether we want to go and see for ourselves; celebrity profiles bring us a bit of vicarious glamour; reader-service features offer guidance on practical subjects like cooking, gardening, motoring, fashion and travel. Many feature writing techniques can be applied to all these types of material.

Be sure the feature is topical. Because features are not news doesn't mean they can be timeless. If an intended piece could have run six months ago, or could still run in six months' time, then perhaps we should write about something else. Many potential feature subjects are always around, but a related news event will project them above the horizon into relevance, perhaps irresistibility!

Have an indirect intro. There is usually no merit in starting baldly with the subject of the feature. In this way, feature intros tend to be the opposite of news intros, which try to give the main point in a nutshell. Features are not about points in that sense but about exploring subjects. Most features for most of us are easily avoidable. We need to be coaxed to read. The indirect approach includes mood intros that create an atmosphere; illustrative (or case in point) intros that take a pertinent example to introduce the subject; quotation intros and question intros, where the quote is telling and the question so compelling that we have to read on.

Let intros run. The news intro is the single first paragraph, by which we stand or fall in getting the main information across. A feature intro can be as long as it takes to achieve the desired effect, which is about inviting or intriguing readers into the piece rather than informing them about something. Mood intros and teaser intros, in particular, may be several pars long.

Have a strong ending. The ending of a feature is nearly as important as the intro, but typically receives only a fraction of the attention given to the intro. This is a pity because the ending is a marvellous chance to fix the feature in the reader's mind with an apt quote, a well worded conclusion, a return to the intro point to tie up the package neatly. Coming back to the start is a favourite way of ending a feature: a Guardian article on distractions while driving began with a case in point intro about a driver who had a fatal accident when trying to adjust his radio. Several hundred words later and after quoting the advice of safety experts, writer Danny Lee ended: "However, as Fiona Jones [the widow] knows all too well, even the simplest of tasks that takes a driver's mind off the road can have terrible consequences." The choice of outro is ours – but go out strongly. Usually avoid ending with a question. We've just slogged through 1,200 words to find some answers, not more questions.

Complain if the feature is cut from the bottom. In a well constructed feature cuts for length need to be taken from the middle. To cut from the bottom means taking out the ending, which should be integral to the piece. With news stories, which are structured differently, it is normally possible to cut from the bottom, and that is probably where confusion arises.

Explain, explain, explain. It is easy to overestimate readers' background knowledge, even in specialist publications. Professional shipbuilders as a group may know little about roll on-roll off ferries in particular. If in doubt about including background explanation, put it in. Sometimes writers fear that readers will feel talked down to, but it is far more likely that readers will be annoyed by background information being left out. Defensive words and phrases like "obviously" and "of course" weaken the piece. If we feel information ought to be included, even if for a minority of readers, we should include it without apologising for doing so.

Follow the rule of three for sources in news features. A single quoted source, however authoritative, is not enough to carry a news feature. As an examination of a topical subject, a news feature needs at least two and properly three identified sources, named if possible, if it is to carry conviction.

Take a personal stand. A feature is more likely to fail because we underproject ourselves than because we overdo it. It's the other side of the editorial equation from news, where we avoid "editorialising" (expressing personal views). Editorials and personal columns, by contrast, should express clear opinions. Articles about gardening and cookery may be enlivened by the information that the writers hate azaleas or love the lowlife favourite of Yorkshire pudding with floating gravy. Even news features properly offer a personal perspective on the subject; otherwise they read like extended news stories.

Go with the flow. The writing style of a feature is necessarily more complex than that of a news story. As a vehicle for information, the news story makes a series of statements. It can be quite staccato. Flow is of no particular importance, although we want to avoid jerkiness. A feature involves weaving together a sequence of ideas and sources, and flow becomes more important. Simple transition words like "yet", "although", "another" or "and" will help. Watch, too, for a sequence of thought that readers find natural. A helicopter jump without warning from one part of the forest to another will not help them keep up with us.

Leave a feature to settle. Writing ENDS and then immediately sending in the material is almost guaranteed to produce a less effective piece than could have been. This especially refers to the flow. Ideally, a feature will be left to stand overnight, but even an hour away from it helps. Looking at the piece again, we may see better sequences of pars, better ways to link points. Even worse, factual errors may come leaping off the screen. This way at least we catch them in time.

5 Freelance Contributions

FREELANCING provides many opportunities for journalists throughout newspapers and magazines, and beyond. Yet it remains a hard way to make a living. Freelances feel they have to be constantly on call. Fees of £400-£500 for a 1,000-word article are not uncommon – although, regretfully, fees of a quarter of that are even commoner! – but the arithmetic is still against being able to make a living from freelance journalistic writing. For most people, freelancing is a part-time activity or is supplemented with other media activities. These include shifts on newspapers and magazines, and public relations work. Freelance agencies that provide coverage of particular towns and areas for the national news media can be very profitable. They deal in news, which can be supplied to many clients at the same time. Features are less attractive financially because they can be supplied only to one outlet, at least in the same form [see Milk The Cow later in the chapter]. The agencies are usually well established, and an incoming freelance would find it hard to compete.

Make contact before submitting an article. Anybody with an idea for an article and the ability to write it should feel free to approach newspapers and magazines. It is not a good idea to send unsolicited material, however. It may well be ignored or overlooked. If a piece is not suitable for the particular publication, we want to know quickly so we can offer it elsewhere. Although most people find making "cold contact" hard, the best way is to phone up and see if they are interested. In a national newspaper a feature might potentially suit three or four different sections, each doing its own commissioning. If our idea is not right for the people we're talking to, they might suggest who else to approach. We might simply be invited to send in the article for consideration. Or we might be invited to send an outline [synopsis].

Give minimum information in outlines. The aim in writing an outline is to give enough information to persuade the client to look at the article, but no more. Theft of ideas, where the idea is given to a staff person or to a favoured freelance, is not common but it happens. In particular, we should not be too specific about whom we will contact as sources for the article. Contacts are valuable resources for journalists, to be guarded carefully.

Be clear about commissioning. A commission is a contract, written or spoken, to produce a specified article for the publication concerned. The act of ordering the material commits the client to pay for it [see below] although not necessarily to use it. Being invited to send in a piece, particularly in response to our offering it, is not the same as being commissioned, and the client has agreed to nothing except looking at the material. Unless we are a household name or a famous expert, no-one is going to commission somebody who phones in with an idea. Commissioning usually comes later, when they have got to know us. The magic moment for freelances is when the client starts to phone them! Editors will only invite us to send an outline or an article if it seems promising so that is a good stage to reach.

Resist 'kill fees'. A commissioned piece may not be used because it has been overtaken by events, or simply squeezed off the list. The piece must still be paid for and, since neither circumstance is the writer's fault, the British Association of Journalists and others hold that it should be paid for in full. The habit of 50% "kill fees" breaches long-standing industry best practice. If the piece is for some reason sub-standard, then we should be willing to agree a reduced fee – although we ought to have been given the chance to rectify faults before the piece is dumped. Sadly, it is not unknown for an editor to claim a piece is sub-standard as an excuse to pay a 50% kill fee!

Be clear about copyright. The first job of a new freelance is to get published rather than get involved in a copyright wrangle, which could sink the sale. Somewhere down the line, however, we may need to protect our interests through an awareness of copyright. Under English law the copyright in a freelance article remains the contributor's unless he or she has transferred it to the client publication. If it has not been transferred, the publication is buying only the right to first use in its medium (print periodicals). This is the case whether the article has been commissioned or submitted speculatively. The copyright owner is able to make further use of the material, for example by republishing it, selling it to other newspapers and including it in a book. British newspapers and magazines, which also have their web versions to consider, are increasingly keen to take full copyright. Although in strict law the copyright transfer needs the active agreeement of the writer, in practice few freelances are in a position to resist a publication that simply declares it has bought the copyright.

Be aware of syndication. The wish of publishers to take full copyright in an article is not mainly about the worldwide web, where it is claimed web publication falls within the basic print permission, but about syndication. British national newspapers and many magazines have elaborate arrangements to sell on material internationally and also to other UK publications. Freelances may get a share of these syndication profits, although some publications don't pay any extra, arguing that the putative benefits are included in the original fee. This syndication network makes it difficult for a freelance to re-sell the material even where he or she has held on to the copyright. That's why well established freelances may sell an article to a publication without syndication rights, or with geographical restrictions so they can sell the material in those countries themselves.

Milk the cow more than once. With copyright in articles publishers hold most of the cards, but the freelance still has the source material. Copyright exists in the words used. Since there is no copyright in ideas, subjects and information, the freelance is free to re-arrange that material to exploit it with other outlets. Hence the saying, An article is not sold if it's sold only once! The sensible freelance keeps some of the material back so that a later article is more than a reshuffling of words and facts; it also contains new information.

Don't be afraid to ask for expenses. Editors may be surprisingly receptive to the idea of expenses as well as the fee – provided the request is made in advance. Editors don't like faits accomplis – who does? They expect us to absorb a normal amount of telephoning, or travel in our immediate area, but if we face a lot of long distance or overseas calling or a long journey, we should certainly ask for this to be covered financially.

Don't leave features hanging around. In the editor's electronic in-tray, that is. Because features, unlike news, have to be offered exclusively, we can't afford to have an idea hanging around until its topicality has gone, and with it its saleability. We are entitled to a decision within days rather than weeks – or hours with hot material. If necessary, we should withdraw the material ourselves if a decision is too drawn out, and move on to the next and hopefully better prospect.

Find out how fees are paid. Some newspapers and magazines, particularly the large ones, produce payments without invoices (known as self-billing). This is a convenient system for the hard-pressed freelance with little time for admin or the means of checking where material has appeared. Other publications will wait for our invoice, which means we must have checked how much to bill for. Late payments are the biggest freelance complaint. We need to keep track of payments owed, to be sure that the self-billing system has worked or that our invoice has been processed with due speed. English law, being progressively extended to businesses of all sizes, requires payments to be made within 30 days of invoicing. After that, creditors may charge interest. While few freelances will care, or dare, to invoke the law, it is a handy benchmark of what can be reasonably be expected. It gives us a basis for chivvying clients into paying up.

6 Press Releases and Advertorial

THE press release, which perhaps should be called news release since the media include broadcasting and the internet, is the workhorse of active media relations. More elaborate and more targeted approaches have their place, but the press release gets information into the public domain widely and cheaply. Although press releases have grown into a huge industry, many journalists feel the standard is still low.

Appearance is crucial. Busy news organisations see scores of press releases a day, so it's no surprise that the handful of really well presented ones stand out like bikinis on a nudist beach, and just as agreeably. A well designed logo and good use of colour help, but in hard copy (rather than emailed or on a website) the biggest problem is a crowded appearance – lines too close together, too many lines on the page, the text surrounds [margins and cut-off areas] too small. It may be a fear of sending too many pages, but that is an unnecessary worry. Journalists don't dislike a five-page press release as such, but do tend to dislike a single story that rambles on for five pages. Break that up into two pages of the story and three pages of further information under the heading Notes for Editors, and everybody will be happy.

Write the press release like a news story. This classical advice is based on the fact that many publications are looking for material they can use more or less unaltered. Larger publications are more likely to treat press releases as tip-offs, doing their own follow-ups, but when a substantial newspaper or magazine uses the release "as is" that's bingo! The issuer of the press release not only gets mentioned but also controls the way in which the message comes out. A press release that is too overtly pluggy reduces its chances of being used like this, or perhaps at all. Too much plugging is a common problem. A more subtle approach may produce better results. Another reason to structure press releases like news stories is that hard-pressed editors and specialists warm to a clear headline, a crisp intro and so on in the same way that readers do.

Different strokes for different folks. Most organisations could target their press releases better, reflecting the needs of different groups of recipients. Some of these groups may prefer press releases written differently. In the era of computers and easily interchangeable text, it is amazing that all media users usually get the same press release. The media's needs are diverse – everything from "rip and read" radio needing items of two or three sentences to specialised magazines prepared to treat the subject at length. Sending everyone the same press release guarantees that many won't use it as sent, and at best will treat it as a news tip. National newspapers and major regional dailies hardly if ever use a press release as it stands. For them it may be more effective to present the material as raw information rather than a written-up text. Their reporters may feel they can get to grips with the information more readily that way.

Make access easy. However the press release is presented, it is vital to have contact names and phone numbers for follow-up inquiries. Email contact addresses are also desirable although not a replacement for phone numbers. It's no good giving only nine to five numbers. Journalists, particularly on national papers, frequently work later. Out-of-hours contact arrangements are needed, whether that is somebody who doesn't mind being called at home, or people taking turns to be on call or a voice mail that is frequently checked. The media are always keen to reach the big cheeses, the doers and the deciders. For major announcements, to list the chief executive or a senior director as a press contact will be well received. We then have to ensure that the luminary frees enough time to actually take the calls!

Improve the quality of quotes. Probably the weakest part of the content in most press releases is the direct quotes. Newspapers and magazines use quotes for their vividness and impact; press release writers take the opportunity to try out the latest business jargon, re-state company platitudes or say nothing at all of substance (it's safer that way). Much of the problem is that the quotes are decided beyond the press office by people who don't understand PR needs. They are literally speaking for themselves, not for the media or media users. A British government agency was reliably reported to have a policy of quoting its staff in order of seniority. Where more than one person featured in a press release, they would be quoted according to rank regardless of the news value of what each said. It is commonplace for press releases involving government ministers to start with a quote from the minister even though a quote is not usually the best way to start a news story. Neither habit encourages editors to use that press release.

Keep headlines single line. A single line of all-capitals headline across an A4 page typically allows eight words of reasonable length. This length also looks good in screen displays. It is easily enough to allow us to write an informative headline. It is more effective to keep the head to a single line and not run over into a second line. Headlines for press releases, with rare exceptions, should be straight. Jokey or teaser headlines are risky. Teaser heads may turn people off reading the release, while hard-boiled editors have probably heard all the jokes before. In any case, they like to do the jokes.

Make contact before not after sending a press release. It is a myth that journalists bin press releases unread. The business is too competitive for people to dare do that. It is true that releases are examined and judged very rapidly, which is why a high standard of content and presentation is so important. Most journalists strongly dislike follow-up phone calls from press offices and PR agencies asking Did you get our press release? or Have you decided if you're going to use it? Journalists feel able to decide about usage without nudges and tweaks from outside. A more acceptable approach is to phone up just before the press release is issued, calling attention to something special. This should be done only for special stories otherwise it too will cause annoyance.

The web is not enough. As a way of getting press releases to the media user, websites are a valuable resource but they supplement rather than replace the other methods of distribution. This is because the media user has to choose to access a website, and few can be optimistic that their clients will do that often enough! The art of the press release is to persuade people to use something they didn't know they wanted. Journalists differ about whether they prefer press releases by email or by hard copy. Presumably email will eventually win out, although that can't be certain. Strangely, snail mail [postal] or courier deliveries probably have more future than fax. All the benefits of colour graphics and logos are lost on fax, and we cannot send book or pamphlet material to accompany the press release. Accompanying material – which on a website can be displayed with hot links to the press release – is popular with journalists. Fax is already looking obsolete as a way to deliver press releases.

Send two copies to major news outlets. Perhaps an email to the specialist reporter and hard copy to the news desk, or just hard copies to both. Duplication to the news desk is a safeguard. If the specialist reporter is away, the news desk still has the story. If the reporter is around, the news desk will refer its version to the reporter (who will then have two). Either way, no-one will be offended.

Give advertorials the 'Nescafe effect'. The holy grail of advertising is for people to enjoy an ad in the same way that they enjoy a programme or an article. On British television this was famously achieved by the series of ads showing romance developing over cups of coffee. Advertorial is editorial-style material with an advertising purpose [see chapter Advertising Issues], which may be written by newspapers and magazines or supplied from outside for use in those papers and magazines. An advertorial hopes to achieve the "Nescafe effect". To have a chance, it must be interesting in itself and not just an extended plug for bathroom improvements, foreign travel, complementary medicine or whatever. Advertorials are mainly features. They can be structured like an editorial feature, described earlier. Footnotes, sidebars [p97] and standfirsts [p101] are all places where the promotional message can be underlined.

7 How to Display Quotes

THE actual words people use, called direct quotes, are a vital part of making a news report or feature article come to life. Summarised remarks, or paraphrases, have the advantages of brevity and directness but are not enough, except in the briefest of stories. Most of the examples of direct quotation that follow are based on a remarkable story in the Daily Mail in which otherwise normal seals appeared with orange fur. The experts were stumped, but finally guessed that algae-like creatures had invaded the fur.

Introduce a quoted sentence with a full colon (:). A colon puts emphasis on what follows, so it is more impactful than a comma as a way of introducing the quote:

Stuart Whatley, who was the first to photograph the seals, said: "They are ...

Usually put who said it before what he or she said. The natural place for attribution is at the start of the passage not in the middle or at the end. But it gets boring for every other paragraph to begin "Mr Smith said". Attribution can be moved around for variety.

Use open quote marks for each paragraph of a continuous quote, but use the close quote only at the end.

Stuart Whatley, who was the first to photograph the seals, said: "They are staggeringly orange.

"They look alien really, and show up like fisherman's buoys in the water.

"The only other difference is that they seem more sensitive [to the feel of the rocks] than other seals."

If the quote is a complete sentence, the full stop comes within the close quote marks.

"They look alien really, and show up like fisherman's buoys in the water."

If only part of a sentence is quoted, the full stop comes after the close quotes.

Mr Whatley said the seals "show up like fisherman's buoys in the water".

Attribution within quotes is followed by the same punctuation that the sentence would have taken without it, usually a comma or a full stop.

> *They are staggeringly orange," said Stuart Whatley, who was the first to photograph the seals. "They look alien really." [The attribution comes between sentences.]*

BUT

> *"They look alien really," said Stuart Whatley, who was the first to photograph the seals, "and show up like fisherman's buoys in the water." [The attribution comes within the sentence.]*

Use double quote marks. Many designers have argued for years that traditional speech marks are fussy and single quote marks (') are enough. This convention has become all but universal in UK book publishing, but has made little headway in British newspapers and magazines. It's a visual matter: double quote marks (") show up better and signal the quote more strongly.

Quotes within quotes take the opposite speech mark. If we are using double quote marks, internal quotes are signalled with single quote marks, and vice versa.

> *The witness said: "The robber jumped out from behind a bush and told me, 'Your money or your life'."*

Note the position of the full stop between the two quote marks. The interior quote, whether a full sentence or not, is only part of the main sentence being quoted. The punctuation conforms to the rule mentioned above for quoting parts of sentences.

Go easy on ... The use of three dots between quoted words is a scholarly device to indicate that words have been taken out (usually for brevity and clarity). Trouble is, in journalism it raises a credibility gap: readers wonder just what has been left out! Quote marks are our pledge to readers that what is quoted is what was said. We have to be very careful about dropping bits from inside direct quotes. If it doesn't alter the sense, it may be all right to do this with the flannel that appears in many press releases. A better way may be to "write around" the obstacle, as shown below.

These are the original remarks: *"Mostly racism is unwitting, but there are some church members who deliberately obstruct. The church is not made up of perfect people, but of people who need to be perfected. Separate groups are not separatist. Women have their own church groups. Similar considerations apply for black people."*

We need to shorten the quote. Here is one way: *The minister said: "Mostly racism is unwitting, but there are some church members who deliberately obstruct ... Separate groups are not separatist. Women have their own church groups. Similar considerations apply for black people."*

A better way may be to approach it as two quotes, removing the need for the three dots. Quoting part of a sentence can help here: *The minister said racism was mostly unwitting "but there are some church members who deliberately obstruct". She argued: "Separate groups are not separatist. Women have their own church groups. Similar considerations apply for black people."*

Use single quotes in headlines. Regardless of whether our house style is for double or single quote marks in text, quotes in headlines use single quotes. It's a display thing. Double marks really do look fussy, and belong to the era when full stops were put at the end of headlines.

Tight Writing

TIGHT writing is one of the greatest journalistic virtues. Overwriting reduces the impact of a piece. Fears are sometimes felt that attacking waffle is to drain colour from a piece, but that is a needless worry. It's like saying a garden bush that has run wild is the most elegant example of its type. Good writing comes from the robustness and appropriateness of its language, and from the ideas and images it evokes.

Attack redundant words. Some words attach themselves to others to form time-honoured expressions, yet actually add nothing. In *appointed to the post of chairman* and *cost the sum of £50*, chairman is a post and £50 is a sum of money; therefore the underlined words are redundant. The same is true of *new recruits*, *gave birth to a baby boy* and heaps more.

Attack cliches. Cliches are expressions that were once fresh and vivid, but now have become stale from overuse. We don't have to add to the pile of corn. Among many others, *bolt from the blue, get the green light, red rag to a bull, nipped in the bud* and *up in arms* are expressions that should be pensioned off. Some cliches are merely tired expressions, like *cherished belief* and *mercy dash*, but others are figurative expressions, like *leaving no stone unturned* or *selling like hot cakes*. A cliche in the second sense is still okay for us when it has a literal as well as a figurative meaning, so that it becomes a play on words: "The writing was on the wall for poster artist Fred Brown when he was late for work again."

Attack waffle. Some of the waffle that wanders into our writing has been picked up from the sources we deal with, who evidently feel that long-windedness makes a statement more important: for example, *to give consideration to, was exceeding the speed limit* and *suffered serious injuries*. In plain English these simply mean *to consider, was speeding* and *was badly injured*. We can also cut down waffle by simplifying some grammatical constructions: *despite the fact that* is the same as *although*, *at present* means *now* and *in order to* can often become just *to*.

[The three elements of loose writing described above have been usefully summed up as Passengers, Parasites and Piffle – the Three P's – by the Thomson Foundation, the Cardiff-based journalism study centre. Passengers are the redundant words, parasites are the cliches and piffle is waffle.]

Prefer the shorter alternative. English is rich with synonyms, and there is plenty of scope to find shorter alternatives: *discussions* becomes *talks*, to *initiate* is to *start*, and *conveyed by road* is better as *sent by road*. There are literally hundreds of choices. Many synonyms in English derive from the Norman Conquest, which brought in Norman French, a language based on Latin. In time, this merged with the existing Germanic language of England to form the present language.

Watch words with three or more syllables. The more words with three or more syllables, the harder the passage will be to read. It helps readability if we comb through a piece looking for ways to lower the high-syllable count. Many official documents are full of long words and need to be translated. The three-syllable count excludes verb endings: *harassing* does not count because the root is *harass*; *embarrassing* does count. It can be better to use two or three short words rather than one long one: *participate* is an ugly long word. We are better off with *take part in*.

Often leave out 'that'. The word "that" can often be left out after a verb, particularly "said": *he said (that) he would come on Sunday, she explained (that) she could not come until Tuesday.* Our ears are the best guide. It does not sound quite right to leave out *that* after "added": *they added that they would come as soon as possible.*

Call a spade a spade. Both business and officialdom have developed a vocabulary of euphemisms which we should not buy into. Prices are rarely *raised*, they are *adjusted*. In most contexts, *anti-social behaviour* is a politically correct way of saying *vandalism*. The plain language not only is more communicative but also tends to be shorter.

Use abbreviated names and references. "FSA", "the society" and the like – but only after giving the full name at the first mention unless we are certain our particular readership will know the abbreviation. For a general newspaper, only a handful of institutions, like the BBC, do not need to be spelt out first time. In a business publication, CBI [Confederation of British Industry] would not need spelling out; in a general newspaper it would. FSA? It's the Financial Services Authority. Abbreviations don't refer only to names, and here we need to be even more careful about spelling out their meanings. MBO [management buyout] is a common term in business circles, but in most publications would have to be spelt out first time.

Go easy on jargon. Probably every group of people, from a small-town stamp collecting society to the mighty Ministry of Defence, develops its own jargon, which is a useful shorthand for communication. Trouble is, the rest of us don't know the shorthand. Jargon isn't all bad. Some is vivid and self-explanatory, and we can be happy about using this. But much jargon is neither vivid nor self-explanatory. In the worlds of social work and the theatre, *sectioning a patient* [committing a patient involuntarily to a mental hospital] and *corpsing* [laughing unintentionally as an actor on stage] are well known bits of jargon, but for readers outside those worlds the jargon should be avoided.

Study the Sun and the Mirror. The reporters and subeditors on the Sun and the Mirror are experts at producing tight, clear writing. At their best, we won't find a word out of place or a word too many. Journalism of this standard is too good to be restricted to the mass market. Wherever we are working, we can learn from it. Sadly, these papers sometimes show a fondness for cliche words and expressions, which helps to keep these weary expressions in use.

9 House Style

HOUSE style refers to the consistent way of presenting information like dates, weights and measures, and spellings where the dictionary allows alternatives. Although each matter is small in itself, it is the small things that readers notice. Different ways of presenting dates, for instance, give a ragged, unprofessional feel to the publication.

Identify preferred spellings. The dictionary is full of words that can be spelt in two ways, among them inquire/enquire and judgment/judgement. We have to settle on one way, and stick to it. Some cities, countries and regions have alternative spellings, including Chechnya/Chechenia. This is a separate issue from British and American spellings, where UK readers would look askance if we start using color, center and defense. We can keep American spellings for the names of US organisations, like the Department of Defense and Department of Labor but, referred to descriptively (not the actual name), they become the American defence department and the US labour department.

Identify banned usages. Pedants love spotting inappropriate words and expressions. Trouble is, yesterday's mistake is today's commonplace. Few people are bothered by using contact as a verb ("Contact me after the weekend"), although this was banned by a leading British national newspaper within memory (on the grounds that contact existed only as a noun). Even so, a house style file should include a list of banned usages. Some are just wrong, like infer in the sense of "suggest" (it should be imply). Others bow too deeply to political correctness, like describing schoolchildren – especially those at primary school – as students rather than pupils. The spread of the internet has given currency to American usages that remain alien at least to older British readers, and may be better avoided, including elevator, envision, real estate and vacation.

Count to ten – or 10. The single digit numbers are spelt out (except when used with an abbreviated unit of measurement: seven miles but 7km), and larger numbers are given in figures. Some newspapers and magazines use ten, others 10. It really doesn't matter so long as we choose one style and stay with it. Big generalised amounts are treated similarly: a population of seven million (we are not stating the precise population of 7,092,615), a cost of £7 million (£ being an abbreviated unit of measurement). We may want to simplify million and billion amounts as, eg, £7m, £7bn.

Weigh the style with units of measurement. The innocuous piece of information 7km can be presented in many other ways: 7kms, 7 km, 7 kms, 7km., 7kms. 7 km., 7 kms. are all possible. The same applies to other weights and measures abbreviations. The styles with full points can be discarded as dated, leaving four to choose from. The style given first, 7km, is perhaps neatest, but it's not "righter" than the others.

Keep clear about capitals for titles. The hardest area of house style is capitalisation of titles. Almost all would agree on the Queen, but Honorary Assistant Secretary of the Clackworthy Horticultural Society looks fussy. Yet both are titles. Where do we draw the line? House style has to tackle the issue. One way is to draw that line immediately below the Queen, with everyone else from the prime minister and the archbishop of Canterbury downwards given their titles in lower case. It's even consistent to do the Queen (and the Pope) that way: they are in a different situation from all the others. Even at the first mention we don't have to use their names; the title is enough. So the capitalisation stands in place of the capitalised name.

Keep it consistent with capitals. Capitals are correctly used for the actual names of organisations whether mighty or minute – the Financial Services Authority, Oxfordshire County Council, Clackworthy Horticultural

Society. Shorter references need not take caps: at later mention in the story, it is the authority (or the FSA), the council, the society. An Oxfordshire newspaper that has no need to identify which county council is being written about could refer from the beginning to the county council (lower case). However, names, particularly geographically linked ones, can also be seen as descriptions of the organisations. It is therefore correct to refer to Oxfordshire county council, Clackworthy horticultural society (lower case). To write of the financial services authority would be too strong for the taste of most readers, and should be avoided. Whichever capitalisation style is preferred, the important thing is to keep usage consistent from story to story, page to page. With trade-marked and other proprietary names, capitalisation is not a question of house style but a requirement. If we don't we may get a stiff letter from the company reminding us of its trademark. Any old 4x4 is not a land rover. Land Rover has to be capitalised, and used only when the vehicle really is one.

What to do about dates. Of the many possibilities for writing a date, the commonest journalistic style is December 25. By tradition, a year if included has commas both before and after, but there has been a trend to simplify by writing, eg, August 10 2000 will always...

What's the point of points? Many newspapers and magazines have stopped using points with abbreviations on the basis that they look fussy and aren't needed. It's a long time since many people wrote B.B.C. Points with Mr., Mrs., Dr., Rev. etc are still seen, but visually are just as redundant. It's sensible to leave out the point from units of measurement like km and lb, and abbreviations like etc and eg.

Stay singular. Bodies like councils, committees, associations and societies can be seen as singular or plural. The usual style is to treat them as singular: the council has decided etc. Sports teams, however, are invariably treated as plural (whether they play as a team or as an assortment of individuals!): Manchester United are magic (or insert team of choice).

Be entitled. The titles of books, plays, films, newspapers and so on are variously quoted, set in italic or bold types, or left unquoted in plain type. The most popular style is the simplest – plain type unquoted – but as a matter of house style the choice is ours.

10 | Language Traps

TECHNICALLY correct English is an issue that concerns some readers greatly and leaves others unmoved. As writers we are the pig in the middle. Our best course is to lean towards strict usage. Some language mistakes show amazing powers of survival in journalism.

Better/best. Best refers to three or more. We can't have the best of two possibilities. Comparison of two requires better: *it's better to take the train than the car*.

Missing second comma. One of the uses of the comma as a punctuation mark is to signal supplementary passages in a sentence, especially with which and who. A good rule of thumb is that if we use a comma at the start of an inserted passage we also need another one at the end (or a full stop if the passage also ends the sentence). *The Battle of Hastings, which was fought in 1066 is a defining moment in English history. John Brown, who is married with two children is moving on.* Both are incorrect: we need a comma after 1066 and children respectively. If a statement makes sense without the words in question we need two commas; if it doesn't we need none. *He who laughs last laughs longest* would be meaningless without the words governed by who, and needs no punctuation within the sentence.

Unnecessary comma in a series. *Three cheers for Tom, Dick, and Harry*. The final comma in a series (ie after Dick), although classically correct, can be left out because and serves the same purpose. Occasionally the final comma is needed to avoid ambiguity: *men, women and children with medical certificates*. Is it everybody who needs medical certificates or just the children? *Men, women, and children with medical certificate*s makes clear (or fairly clear – arguably constructions like this should be rewritten) that only the children need certificates.

Mismarked possessive. An apostrophe is used to show possession and normally follows the rule: singular 's, plural s'. *Sarah's book*. *The girls' books*. Any chief subeditor would be rich if he or she had a pound for every erroneous use of *womens'*, *childrens'* and *peoples'*. The s' rule does not apply for plural words that don't end in s. *Women* (not *womens*), *children* (not childrens) and *people* (not *peoples* except as *peoples of the world*) are plural words, and the possessive is shown by 's: *women's rights, children's clothes, the people's William* [W.E. Gladstone].

Hardy perennials. The pronoun is *its – every dog has its day*. *It's* is the contraction for *it is*. It's *neither ... nor* and *either ... or*. So a sentence like "It's neither one thing or the other" is grammatically neither one thing nor the other. Hanging participles are words that are not related properly to the main part of the statement. *Beaten to the top job, John's prospects were poor. Enjoying a challenge, mountaineering was Susan's favourite sport. Walking through a dark alley, the gang mugged the couple.* "Beaten" refers to John, not his prospects; it wasn't mountaineering that was "enjoying" the challenge, it was Susan; "walking"only makes sense as a reference to the couple rather than the gang. So hanging, or dangling, participles mean ugly or unclear sentences. It's usually a simple matter to rewrite sentences to avoid them.

Wandering 'only'. 'Only' tends to wander around in sentences, but for the best effect it is placed next to the words it refers to. *The Settle-Carlisle railway was only saved after public pressure* is poorly expressed because only doesn't somehow limit saved but refers to the public pressure. *The Settle-Carlisle railway was saved only after public pressure* is better.

The vanishing hyphen. The virtual disappearance of hyphens from many newspapers and magazines is in some ways welcome. Fussiness is not a service to readers. This punctuation mark still has its uses, however. One is to avoid ambiguity. *After the Battle of Borodino the Russian army was able to re-form* means that the soldiers could reassemble after the battle. *After the Battle of Borodino the Russian army was able to reform* means that administrative systems were changed, promotions were awarded on merit and so on! Where two of the same vowels come together a hyphen makes the word easier to read: *co-operative* (not *cooperative*), *re-elect* (not *reelect*). Hyphens are also useful as a readability aid for nouns formed of more than one word: a *seven-year-old* (not *seven year old*), the *commander-in-chief* (not *commander in chief*).

Symmetrical expression. *Borodino was fought between the Russians and French*. For smoothness, it should be *the French*. *The party comprised a Scot, two Germans and a Danish soldier*. This is worse because it leaves journalistic loose ends as well as being inelegant. What are the occupations of the Scot and the two Germans? Why single out the Dane in this way? (Comprised is correct, not comprised of.)

Gender-free language. There is an understandable reaction against sexist language where all the world seems to be male. *Every homeowner should see that he is* *well insured* takes no account of the fact that vast numbers of homeowners are women and, perhaps even worse, stereotypes homeowners as male. Many will now write *Every homeowner should see that they are well insured* – explicitly to get round the gender issue. Yet the proper answer cannot be to fracture the language by joining a plural pronoun (they) with a singular noun (homeowner). The problem can usually be written round, most easily by making the subject plural (*all homeowners*, which makes they correct). Where it can't, as in places in this book, there are worse things to write than his or her. An amusing idea to overcome the problem is to use the arbitrary word *co* wherever he or she and his or her are needed in conventional English: *Every homeowner should see that co is well insured*. It would work, but so far the typical English speaker has not shown that co is much interested. With far less reason, singular and plural are often mixed when writing about councils, associations and societies. *The council has decided they cannot afford to repair the road. They* should be *it* for the sentence to be consistent.

Problem words. Accommodation, embarrass, harass and supersede are four of the most commonly misspelt words. They are correct here! Principal means chief and principle refers to theory or morals. Disinterested means impartial and is often wrongly used instead of uninterested. To insure means to arrange compensation for possible future loss and ensure means to make certain. The government licenses (verb) cars and motorists hold licences (nouns). Forbear is to refrain from something, forebear is an ancestor. To gather together, particularly troops, is to marshal. Marshall exists only as a name, although the past tense of marshal is marshalled. Complement makes complete (mint sauce complements lamb, a ship's complement) and compliment expresses appreciation. Homogenous, which refers to common descent, is usually intended to mean made up of similar parts, uniform, and should be homogeneous (a homogeneous culture). There are, sadly, plenty more.

11 | Arts Reviews

REVIEWS of books, plays, films, concerts and exhibitions command much space in many newspapers and magazines. Reviewers are among the publication's best known bylines, sometimes even acquiring a personal following. The purpose of an arts review is only secondarily to guide readers on whether to buy it or watch it themselves: most readers will never experience the art event themselves.

Tell a story. Because most readers will not read the book or attend the event they are not looking for a chapter-by-chapter, scene-by-scene or movement-by-movement appraisal of the work. Nor is a review a precis. Many people read reviews just to keep in touch with the world of arts. A review should read interestingly for its own sake.

Don't give away the ending. Some readers, even if a minority, look to the review for guidance on whether to read the book, watch the play or film, go to the concert or visit the exhibition. With most films, plays and fiction books, readers' pleasure will be spoilt if the ending is given away. It may even be destroyed. Someone may give the book or film a miss because the reviewer has said too much. Regrettably, giving away the ending is a habit that seems to have spread among reviewers.

Make a judgement. However interesting the story or fascinating the incidents, a reviewer ought not duck the challenge of judging the work. How good (or bad) is it? How does it compare with comparable works may also be relevant. The need for judgement is a reminder to us all to avoid doing reviews in areas where we know little!

Name names. In films and professional theatre answer what is often the reader's first question – who's in it? – by mentioning the main performers early in the article. With amateur play productions the days should be long gone when we mentioned every actor, and quite a few of the behind-scenes staff, to boost the paper's sales. With am dram it may be kinder to leave some of the lesser performers unmentioned and therefore uncriticised.

Spot the genre. An art event does not occur in a vacuum, and the review should aim to put the particular work into a context. The author, playwright or composer has probably done previous work. How does this one relate to that? Is the film what we'd expect from the leading actor? Directors mainly work in particular genres. How does this compare with others of his/her genre? How does it compare with other people's work in the same genre?

Be a personality. Or at least don't be afraid to let the quirks and hobby-horses show! The more we're seen as a cross between a sage judge and an off-the-wall columnist, the happier the editor (and probably the readers) will be.

12 Proof Correcting

PROFESSIONAL proof-readers are an endangered species now that printers do not have to re-type what the writer has written. With emails and floppy disks, material is sent for typesetting without further keystroking. It means that every writer and certainly every editor has to be his or her own proof-reader. There is plenty of scope to use the proof correction symbols to be found on the British Standard Institution's card BS 5261C: 1976, whether we are checking a hard copy or correcting a page proof.

Mark everything twice on typeset proofs. BS 5261C tells us that for each proof correction instruction a distinct mark is to be made (a) in the text and (b) in the margin. With typeset material this double marking is the only clear way to do it. The lines are so close together that there will be no room to add inserted words between the lines, for example. Or a mark, say a deleted character, might be missed because the type is so small.

Mark changes only once on hard copy. With material in manuscript [copy before it has been keyed into the computer system] or computer printouts, it is usually enough to mark the changes in the text. Because the letters ar larger, alterations are plainly visible, and there will normally be enough space to insert new words between the lines (not in the margin, as we do with typeset material). The fewer the marks, the less chance of confusion in the correcting process.

Make your meaning clear on page proofs. As typeset material the double system of correction is used, but writing in the margin can be a problem when there isn't one! An item in the middle of a newspaper or magazine page, surrounded by other stories, has no obvious edge. So put the mark in the nearest edge, drawing a line between the text mark and the margin mark if there is any room for doubt about what goes where.

Expect to miss errors on screen. So look even harder! Correcting copy on screen has the great advantage of WYSIWYG: what you see is what you get. There is no chance that our marks will be misunderstood because there are no marks and no-one else between us and the completed correction. However, it puts an added weight on us to pick up 100% of the mistakes. Many people feel that it is harder to spot errors on screen than on paper. How we read is affected by familiarity with the medium (screen or paper), self-confidence in the medium and styles of type (some are more easily read than others). There may be something in the feeling, though. The physical definition of characters is not as great on screen as it is on paper, making them harder to read. With a computer screen we are locked into a constant reading position, but with paper we can chop and change the reading angle to make ourselves more comfortable. In another sense, computers should make it harder for mistakes to slip through. The spellchecker will alert you to mistakes even if you missed them. It won't catch the fact that the Battle of Hastings was not fought in 1067, but it ought to mean that you don't spell ACCOMMODATION with one C.

	IN THE TEXT	IN THE MARGIN
INSERT	the best/is	*of all* ⟨
MAKE CAPITAL	in paris	≡
MAKE L.C.	the Ceremony	≢
DELETE single character	zebraa	♪
DELETE multiple characters	a fine baby boy	♪
CLOSE UP	rece ive	⌒
DELETE AND CLOSE UP	recedive	♪
INCLUDE SPACE	here and now	Y
TRANSPOSE	sizze	⊔⊓
PARAGRAPH INDENT	xxxxxxxxxxx	
	xxxx⌐xxxxx	⌐
	xxxxxxxxx	
MAKE ITALIC	a really fine person	⫽⫽
MAKE BOLD	York is a must	∿

Common proof reading marks (based on British Standard 5261C)

13 Copy Editing

COPY EDITING is traditionally subeditors' work, although on large publications much may be done by the news desk before the material reaches the subs. Proof readers too inevitably go beyond their strict role of correcting misprints and spelling errors, and into aspects of copy editing like house style and factual and grammatical accuracy. Copy editing is as much an activity, performed by various people, as a job.

The proof reader suggests, the subeditor decides. Subeditors have a wide authority over the material that proof readers lack. Beyond the core areas of correct spelling and house style, proof readers will raise queries about grammatical and factual accuracy but will not normally make changes on their own account. Subeditors not only can make these changes but also ought to as part of their job. They may also decide to make substantive changes to the material, like changing the order of pars or even creating a new intro. Subeditors tend to give too little attention to editing text, either through timidity or because they are tied up with other aspects of the job.

Edit news harder than features. Subbing changes don't need the approval of the writer. Practice varies from office to office on how much the writer is consulted, ranging from always to never. The extent of editing also varies among publications, with the tabloid national newspapers edited harder than their broadsheet counterparts. News customarily is edited harder than features, with reporters less likely to be consulted about changes than feature writers. Features are more personal creations than news stories so the writer has a stronger claim to be consulted about substantial changes. But in reality a feature writer is more likely to suffer from under-editing than over-editing.

Hold seven areas in mind at once. Easier than it sounds once we have the knack! The subeditor is concerned with factual and grammatical accuracy, house style, tight writing, legal safety, good taste and journalistic impact. It's impracticable to read a piece over seven times, but we have to try to hold all these areas in mind at once as we read. A readover to the end of a piece before we start editing can save time by giving us a better overall view.

If in doubt cut it out. This traditional advice should really be If in doubt check and if you can't find the answer cut it out. It's doubtful if generations of subs would have remembered the advice in that form, however!

Consistency even trumps accuracy. An important job for anyone carrying out the activity of copy editing (news editor, subeditor, proof reader) is to make sure that personal and place names mentioned several times are spelt the same throughout. If they aren't and there is really no way to find out (often the case with foreign stories), we have to proceed on a "best guess" basis. If a name is spelt three times one way and once in another way, it's obvious where to jump. If there are two mentions, spelt differently, we can spin a coin – consistency is that important. We should check all foreign currency conversions where both the original and the pound amounts are given. The same rate of exchange should apply to each amount mentioned. It should be second nature to check any list of percentage amounts that ought to add up to 100 (although 99 or 101 is acceptable allowing for figures rounded up and down). Since reporters are famously bad at arithmetic, it often doesn't! If there is no other way of resolving the difficulty, we can take one item out of the list and use the others after the word "including". At least that way the inconsistency is concealed.

Ensure cuts can be reinstated. We may change our mind. When cutting material to length so that it fits the allocated space, it's quicker to cut freely and reinstate passages than to carefully count the deleted lines as we go. Cuts are easily reinstated if they have been transferred to "notes" mode or similar categories in computer programs; or we can make a copy file before subbing so a passage can be pasted back into the subbed version if needed.

14 Handling Pictures

BIG and dramatic pictures have become part and parcel of newspaper as well as magazine journalism – a style that has its roots half a century and more ago with Picture Post in Britain and Life in the United States. In the 1930s the Daily Mirror was celebrated for its use of pictures while three decades or so later the French-language magazine Paris-Match set an innovatory standard. More recently, UK national broadsheets have out-tabloided the tabloids by using pix in sizes that only their larger format makes possible. These design trends are complemented by the spread of digitised pictures. It is easier to crop and place a pic on-screen than it is to handle a print.

The more off-square a pic, the more dramatic the effect. Pronounced vertical and horizontal shapes are very striking, although they would lose impact if we did every pic like that. A completely square shape is static and should be avoided.

Crop tightly, enlarge generously. This classic tip is as good as ever. Many journalists have taken up the enlargement advice more wholeheartedly than they have the cropping advice. Loose cropping is a common problem, with needless amounts of sky, grass and walls in evidence. Every bit of unwanted background physically reduces the size of the bits we are interested in. It's possible to crop too tightly, however, as several sections below suggest.

See the content in thirds. If we imagine a picture cut into thirds vertically, the liveliest positions for the main content are along those dividing lines. For example, a man sitting at a desk will look better if he is off-centre. The same applies with the horizontal dividing lines. A key feature in the picture is wasted if it is right at the edge of the pic.

Allow space in front of moving objects. The sense of movement in a picture comes from our seeing the object in relation to the background. If all the background is removed around a Formula 1 racing car, the car appears not to be moving. Cropping tightly behind a moving object and leaving space in front for it to move into maximises the sense of movement.

Avoid chopping legs and arms. If a pic has to be cropped for space reasons, it's better to take away the whole arm at the shoulder than to cut it off at the elbow. Same with legs, where a crop at the waist looks better than slicing through the knees. It is often impossible to do this with sports pix, but we can still try.

Make the most of mug shots. The ideal mug [face] shot shows the head, cropped closely up to the ears, and just the beginning of the shoulders. It's all right to take a bit off the top of the head, as if we were slicing a boiled egg, but over-tight crops that show just the face with ears, hair and neck removed are ugly and may be hard to recognise. When mug shots are used together, we should be careful that there is no jarring difference of scale, that the heads are the same size.

Have a pic facing into the page. A picture with a strong sideways thrust – a face in profile or a moving object – needs to be placed so that the direction is into the page. Otherwise the eye is drawn out of the page. We also want the subject matter facing into the text it accompanies, to integrate the two. We may be able to use an awkward picture by reversing the original image, but this is possible only if the pic is free of giveaway features like lettering, coat buttons, wedding rings and chest medals. All these things will be reversed too.

Look for strong contrasts. In monochrome, a highly contrasty pic with strong black and dark grey tones as well as lots of light grey and white will print better and look more interesting than one dominated by middle shades of grey. Colour pix also need to be chosen with thought for the colours as well as the content [see chapter Impact from Colour].

Selection checklist. Too many backs of heads in the audience and among the crowd can make a picture unusable. Features that look fine on the screen or in the glossy may be invisible in low-quality newsprint. "In the background is the railway line." Where? All we see is murk. In captions, we need to mention background content with care. The most important selection consideration is a sense of action: people in a landscape, things moving rather than standing still, groups in action not just sitting or standing for the camera.

Go easy on digital tweaking. Digitised pictures offer almost limitless possibilities for altering content. If a glamour model is perfect in every way except for shortness in the leg, those legs can be extended. Changing the colour of hair or clothes is so routine as to be hardly worth mentioning. New heads can be put on old shoulders, or whole people removed and others added. Indeed, everyone can made to seem somewhere else by changing the background. Picture fakery is probably as old as pictures in journalism. Often it was easy to spot. With digital manipulations it's a lot harder, or impossible. We don't need to deny ourselves the advantages of the technology, but there is a quantum gap between tweaking two figures closer to remove the empy space between them and removing someone from a group shot. Producing a leggier model may not matter because we are dealing in fantasy; to "tidy up" people in news pix is a distortion of real life. We all have to decide how far down this road we are willing to go.

15 Picture Captions

CAPTIONS range from simple labelling of mug shots and straightforward news pix to composite captions referring to several pix, standalone captions – where the caption must tell it all because there is no separate story – and story captions – where there is no caption and the picture identification is worked into the story itself. Captions are usually written by reporters or subeditors, not by photographers, who arguably are the best people to handle them. Sometimes reporters and subs have inadequate information supplied by the photographers, and sometimes captions are not given the attention their importance demands.

Every caption is a selling opportunity. A caption is more than a way of describing a picture. It is a chance to add to the projection of the story of which that pic is a part. Most readers skip most stories. Many look at everything else before they turn to the text. A lively picture caption may be what decides someone to read the story. The caption for a mug shot should not just say *The mayor*. That is an opportunity lost. Add an appropriate line from the story. *The mayor: boyhood dreams fulfilled*.

Keep identification simple. We need to know who's who in a picture, but the traditional *From left to right* is a passenger phrase [see earlier chapter Tight Writing]. If it starts from the left where can it go except to the right? *From left* is better. Other styles of identification can be used as appropriate: *middle row, with glasses*. We should avoid stating the self-evident. *The headmistress (second from right) with award-winning pupils* is unnecessary unless the headmistress is improbably young!

Don't state the obvious. Captions should do more than state what readers can see for themselves in the picture. If Joyce Brown is smiling happily as she receives her long-service gold watch from the managing director, we should find more to say than that Joyce Brown is smiling happily as she etc... Avoid imposing a dubious interpretation of a picture. We may want the bystanders to look horrified – but do they? Watch too for stating the obvious by way of information and explanation. This one slipped into a national newspaper: *A boat is guided through a street at Newton Abbot. The town was hit by floods*. The caption seems to suggest that there are other towns where boats routinely float through streets, not just when there are floods.

Use the present tense. The mayor *plant*s the commemorative oak is faster than the mayor *planting* the commemorative oak. The present tense of the verb has more immediacy than the participle.

Composite captions: uses and abuses. Composite captions are a useful way of describing several related pix in a single block of words, with captions like *Clockwise from above*. The composite caption emphasises the relatedness of the pix. It may also help the page layout to have the captioning in a single block. Composite captions work best when the pix are clustered. If the pix are scattered around the page it may be hard to link a pic with its explanation.

Caption typography. It was once common for captions to be set in italic type, but now they are normally set in bold type. This may be the bold of the text type or a contrasting face, typically a sans type, slightly larger (say 10pt to the text size of 8pt or 9pt), where text is set in a seriffed type. The full stop should be left out at the end of the caption. If the caption has more than one sentence the previous sentences are ended with full stops, but the last sentence remains without

16 Writing Headlines

HEADLINES are arguably the hardest part of the subeditor's work to do well. To express the gist of a complicated situation in five or six words is a knack. Most people with a bit of practice can write pedestrian headlines. Top operators turn in, day after day, headlines at an altogether higher level.

The headline golden rule. A man appeared in an Edinburgh court accused of vandalising St Giles's Cathedral. He had spray-painted an insulting message on the main doors. When asked why he had inappropriately scrawled To Hell With the Pope on this Protestant building, he replied: "Because To Hell With the Moderator of the General Assembly of the Church of Scotland wouldn't fit." This doubtless apocryphal story reminds us that the most brilliant headline is useless if it won't fit in the allocated type size and space. It's also a reminder that on the news pages it's better practice to write headlines to a specified type size and width rather than fit the type to the wording. (In features it is sometimes right to work in reverse, and design the page around an apt headline.)

Use the present tense. Headlines use the present tense of verbs to describe past events for the sake of vividness. The headline says SHIP SINKS but the intro says "A ship has sunk" or "A ship sank yesterday". A head like 'DRIVER DID 80 THROUGH TOWN CENTRE' comes within the present-tense rule. Although the event referred to is in the past tense the quote marks indicate that someone is saying this, and are an alternative to PROSECUTION CLAIMS (present tense).

Leave out 'is', 'are', 'a', 'the'. These articles and auxiliary verbs are normally left out of news headlines for the same reason: vividness. GIRL MISSING has far more punch than A GIRL IS MISSING. Articles and auxiliaries are sometimes kept in feature heads, especially if the line is echoing a well known expression: A ROOM WITH A VIEW.

Prefer a sentence to a label. Verbs are the main word-form to denote action, and we should try to make our headlines active by including a verb. A headline without a verb is called a label. FALKLANDS OIL FIND is a label, lacking life. OIL FOUND IN FALKLANDS is better. The rule should not be seen as absolute, however. Particularly in features it may be better to use a telling expression that lacks a verb; in news a label head may allow us to say more in a tight space.

Prefer an active verb to a passive verb. The verb is active in the headline DIVERS FIND WRECK. It is passive in WRECK FOUND. It's good to seek ways expressing the headline actively, but there are plenty of exceptions. The passive construction is shorter, as the example shows, and may be the only one to fit. The active construction may shift the emphasis inappropriately. The passive head MP CITED FOR CORRUPTION, where the emphasis is on the MP, is stronger than COMMITTEE CITES MP FOR CORRUPTION, where the emphasis is on the committee.

Use quote marks for opinions and claims. The headline SALESMAN 'LURED WIDOW TO DEATH' needs quote marks to indicate that it's a claim somebody is making. (After a guilty verdict the prosecution evidence is taken as fact so the head could appear without the quotes.) The headline 'TRAFFIC BAN BEST FOR TOWN', however much greens might agree, reflects an opinion that others would dispute. It also needs quote marks. Without them it could be read as the publication's own opinion – not appropriate in the news columns. In neither case do we need to specify who is making these statements. It is, however, important to show that they are claims and opinions rather than proved facts. Headlines may also specify the speakers, and then we don't use quote marks:

SALESMAN LURED WIDOW TO DEATH – PROSECUTION

TRAFFIC BAN BEST FOR TOWN, SAY GREENS

Be specific. General wording is the enemy of effective headlining as it is of effective intros. MINISTER SETS OUT POLICIES and MANY HOLIDAY TREATS IN DISNEYLAND are not horribly wrong, but they are below standard because they don't say enough.

Avoid alphabet soup. Too many initials, even of well known organisations, make a headline hard to read (and unpleasant to look at). A good aim is to have just one set of initials per headline. *EU and US back NATO claims to UN* may say a lot, but at a heavy price in readability and elegance.

The main point belongs in the main headline. Headlines with more than one element – ie a main headline and a strapline above or a subline under – should be written so that the secondary line develops the information in the main headline.

Drugs bust nets 50
COURT CHARGES ON WAY

In this pair of headlines the main deck is meaningless without reading the strapline, defeating the purpose of a lead headline. In tabloid journalism, however, there may be a deliberate reversal of content. The main head may be a vivid but probably meaningless phrase like REVENGE OF THE TOFFS, with a strapline or subline used to describe an upper-class mass protest against government action.

Match the headline to the mood of the story. Tragedies or achievements on an epic scale call for headlines that capture the scale of the event. Light headlines are essential for light stories. It isn't easy to be humorous to order with a deadline looming, but the British press has a long tradition of comic headlines, often puns, and nothing less will do. When most hereditary peers were voted out of the House of Lords, the debate was called THE END OF THE PEER SHOW. A feature about an underwater hotel, which guests entered by diving, was headlined HOTEL THAT'S PROUD TO BE A LOW DIVE.

17 How Headlines Look

AS if fitting a complex message or a fun thought into a few words isn't hard enough, the best headlines also look good on the page in terms of type. Perfection we usually can't do, but a few moments' thought can often produce a rewording that turns a poor appearance into a better one

Go easy on squeezing and stretching. This may sound like the exercises we do in the office, but it actually refers to the habit of condensing type to make a line fit or stretching type to make a shy line longer. Handy yes, but you end up with type not looking how God (or designers) made it. Over-condensed type in particular looks horrible. Ideally, we just use type "au naturel" ...

Ditto enlarging or reducing type. Changing the size of headline type to make the words fit better means that we end up with type sizes we never intended. The odd point here or there doesn't make too much difference, but if we do it too often or too much the look of the page is affected. For instance, if a headline is enlarged and the one next to it is reduced, the two become more similar in size and the intended visual distinction is lost.

Be happy with the set left style. Positioning all the lines of a headline with a steady left margin (like text) is the most popular presentation style. Among its virtues is the fact that where lines are short all the white space falls on one side (the right side). White space is a positive element in design so it can be good to emphasise it. When stories are placed side by side the white space helps to separate them.

Be happy with the centred style. There is still mileage in this more traditional way of presenting type. A centred headline has its lines positioned so that the space in a short line is distributed equally between the left and right sides. Because the lines move in and out, the headline looks lively. Where three lines are long, medium and short in descending order, an arrowhead is formed that helps the eye to glide from headline to text.

Mix the two above if you feel like it – but not randomly around a page, which looks messy. Examples of designers getting the best of both worlds include:
- Some sections of the newspaper or magazine set left and others centred.
- Single-column headlines centred and everything else set left.
- Page leads set left and everything else centred.

Always centre boxed and reversed heads (regardless of the style for other headlines). Boxed heads look neater that way, and with reverses the solid background for the lettering is dispersed and does not become too dominating.

Full lines for urgency, airy lines for thought. It all depends what sort of publication you are. Mass market papers often want all lines in a headline to be full. This gives a sense of busy-ness and urgency to the layout. Many other papers and magazines prefer some variety in the length of lines. It slows the design down – and we hope that along with the slower pace comes the feel of thoughtfulness and depth! If we are writing lines of unequal length, we have to follow some ideas about shape, described next.

Make the top line longest. If the top line is shorter than lines below, it draws the eye outwards and away from the text. Only too easy then to avoid reading the story... The top line needn't be full width (provided that it's longer than the other lines), but even so the fuller the better. A single-line head looks much better if completely full.

Beware shy headlines. A shy headline is one that is too short in relation to the available width, and this is probably a higher crime and misdemeanour than producing short top lines. Pages are seriously spoilt by a rash of shy headlines. How short is too short? We can get away with a short line in, say, a four-line headline better than we can in a two-line head. Our eyes suggest that with any sort of headline a line that does not cover half the available width is too shy. It is hoped we will feel an urge to rewrite the head if our first shot fails to reach two-thirds of the width.

Bad breaks are bad news. A bad break is where two or more words that belong together get split between lines. The reader finds them hard to understand – or easy to understand but not with the meaning we intended:

MAYOR SEEKS SEX
SHOP CLOSURE

It may be mythical, but it shows the problem.

18   Page Design

SUCCESSFUL display of editorial material in newspaper and magazine pages involves the interplay of up to six typographical and visual elements: text type, display type, pictures, other visual elements, space and advertisements. Each element needs to be separately considered, and to work in relation to the others. The paradigm style is block (modular) layout, in which every story on the page (including headline and picture if there is one) is arranged as a rectangle. Stories making an irregular shape with columns of different lengths, allowing another story underneath the short first column or a filler after the short last column, look old-fashioned. Apparently easier, modular layout in fact is harder to do well because of the risk of monotony through the repetition of block shapes. Advertisements further limit the chances for varying the blocks. The strictest modular newspapers tend to allow text to leg round ads, creating an angled shape but also avoiding a layout straitjacket. Some newspapers continue to allow banner headlines, in which the head goes across all or most of the page, on top of unrelated material, nowadays invariably a picture. This is not modular, the banner making the main story non-rectangular, but it extends the layout possibilities of the page.

Making a point of size. Type is measured in points, a unit of measurement that in the Anglo-American version is only about one-third of a millimetre (28 1/2 points = 1cm). Such a tiny physical difference in size is still highly visible on the page, say between 8pt and 9pt, two common sizes for text type. Towards the other end of the scale (although sizes go much bigger) 72pt is a large size associated on many publications with page leads. A handy rule of thumb for layout visualisation is that 1cm of depth is needed for every 24 points of headline typography, allowing for spacing. The length of columns of type is stated in centimetres (or inches). The width of a column of type is traditionally expressed in ems, a measurement unit comprising 12 points, but now we often hear type widths spoken of directly in points. A nine-em column is the same as a column of 108 points (9 x 12 = 108). And with the culture of designers replacing that of printers we also hear column widths spoken of in centimetres.

TEXT TYPE
Not too much text type. Cramming in too much text, or body type, is one of the main reasons why pages fail visually. The problem is often acute in sports pages. We can take much less text than we would expect: whatever

the style of layout, if text occupies more than 60% of the available column centimetres (excluding adver-tisements) a bad page is bound to result. An overcrowded layout doesn't allow enough room for headlines, pictures and other forms of display.

Use bold type for contrasts. Bold type, a longtime favourite for boxed stories, is now commonly used for main stories too, positioned to bring contrast to a page. Another popular use is for sidebars [subsidiary stories tied to main stories], where the bold may be set ragged [unjustified] right to contrast with the justified setting of the light (roman) type used in the main story. (Ragged setting is better avoided in boxes.)

Is your italic *really* necessary? There is nothing wrong with italic type, nor with reverse or hanging indent (where the first line of each par is full out and all other lines are indented), although for many years both italics and reverse indent have been out of fashion. No doubt their time will come again.

Wide setting conceals length. Standard column setting emphasises the length of longer pieces, particularly if they run up and down the page. Wider setting makes the material seem shorter and therefore more inviting to read. For this reason newspapers often use a wider setting for features than for news. Magazines commonly run features on a three-column page grid and news on a four-column grid.

Bastard measure is livelier. Bastard measure [setting that is not a multiple of the standard column measure] looks more lively than double column measure. Double column setting is best restricted to short runs, like an intro or a box. A feature running across the top of an eight-column newspaper, for example, is better presented in five or six legs (bastard measure) rather than four (double column).

Avoid the reading 'tennis match'. The maximum acceptable setting width depends on the size of type. If type is presented too wide in relation to its size, readers' eyes have to move backwards and forwards across the lines like spectators at a tennis match. What's acceptable at Wimbledon is not when reading a newspaper or magazine. Optimal reading width has been said to be 1 $1/_2$ alphabets (39 characters). That's less than the typical newspaper double column setting. It suggests that three-column setting is not appropriate except for intros, and even there the style is better avoided.

Type that jumps columns. Many newspapers have followed magazines in allowing discontinuous text type, formerly banned. It used to be felt that for each story type had to form an unbroken ribbon, even if some legs were only three or four lines long. Continuous text is usually still required for the news pages, but with features it may be acceptable, for example, for a centrally placed picture to interrupt the flow of text. The reader leaps from the bottom of one column to the top of the next, across the picture. This allows much bolder layouts. What matters is not a principle called continuous text but whether it is clear where the reader's eye is to go, without hesitation or confusion. A leg of type that ends with a full stop may tell the reader, wrongly, that the article ends there.

DISPLAY TYPE

Display type is type in sizes above those used for body setting, say 14pt upwards. It is used not only for headlines but also for standfirsts, pull quotes, crossheads, drop letters and other effects [see below].

Use sans for impact, serifs for thought. The plain letters of sans typefaces have a bigger visual impact than the more elaborate letters of typefaces with serifs. Roadsigns, where immediate visibility is at a premium, use sans letters. The national "red top" tabloids use sans for headlines while most of the broadsheets use serifs. The red tops want impact and the broadsheets want to suggest thoughtfulness, reflectiveness, reliability. The Guardian in the late Eighties was very radical in breaking with this convention and re-dressing itself with a sans headline type (Helvetica). Even so, in the original redesign the features section was dressed in a particularly thoughtful seriffed type (Garamond). Sans for news and serifs for features is a popular approach, based on the associations of the two type styles.

Text more readable with serifs. The red tops, the Guardian and other users of sans headlines use seriffed type for text because seriffed type is easier to read than sans type in large amounts and in the small sizes used for text (size for size and without extra spacing for sans).

A　A

A seriffed letter (left) and a sans [sans serif] letter. Serifs are the cross strokes on most characters. The seriffed letter is Times and the sans letter is Helvetica – probably the commonest headline typefaces in British newspapers

Use light and bold type for contrasts. The usual way of obtaining contrast among headlines on a page is with bold and light types. Bold italic, formerly used for contrast, has been widely discontinued. The bold and light types may be from the same family, or they may be from different families. If all headlines on a news page are in bold, the effect will bé rather severe. Some light heads are needed for relief. On feature pages, where light heads may be the norm, the opposite applies. In each case, however, one style should be in the majority: a 50:50 split does not send a strong visual signal.

Be sparing with type variety. In the same way that a sweetshop owner doesn't gorge on the sweets, contemporary designers are sparing in their use of different typefaces, although the available choice has never been wider. Newspapers tend to be more sparing in their range of types than magazines. The more upbeat the publication, the more types are likely to be used, but even at the liveliest end the range may be just three or four families (Times is a family), each with several faces (Times Bold, Times Bold Italic and Times Light are faces). It is better to multiply faces than families.

Standfirsts and pull quotes help display. Both standfirsts and pull quotes [words from the article used in small display type] help the layout of a page as well as providing extra hooks to get the reader into the article. A vital use of the pull quote is to relieve a mass of "grey" text type.

Standfirsts 'sell' the article. A standfirst is a trailer for the article it accompanies. More common in features than in news, it can be placed more or less anywhere in an article as the layout requires, including in the middle and to the sides. Below the headline is certainly not the only position. Standfirsts are longer than sub-headlines.

They are written in fully grammatical form, not headlinese where the articles (the, a) and auxiliary verbs (is, are etc) are left out. They usually include the writer's byline. When writing a standfirst, we shouldn't precis the article, but pick a line that is likely to pull readers.

Nothing wrong with crossheads but... The once ubiquitous crosshead is now among the less common ways of breaking up large amounts of text. Other ways include pull quotes and drop letters. A drop letter is a display-sized capital used as the first letter of a word in the text – a style that traces its roots to medieval manuscripts. Popular as a way of starting an article, drop letters can also be used in the middle of articles as breakers. When they are arranged to rise above the text line, a band of white is created alongside the drop cap which enhances the text break.

High-tone effects. Using a tone to print standfirsts, pull quotes and drop letters as grey rather than black gives a pleasing effect and can add welcome variety to a page.

So good we do it to death! Page lead headlines in newspapers that are always the same size and number of lines, or magazine headlines always at the top of the page, become monotonous. Even if the design style is always to use the same size and typeface, we can still vary width, number of lines and position on the page.

PICTURES

Place pictures for balance. Pictures are the most important element for keeping a page in balance, which is a high priority for journalists although not necessarily with graphic designers. A page with the two biggest pictures on the righthand side will be "righthand heavy" and will not look well.

Related pix can cluster. Placing related pix together tends to magnify the impact of the content; it is also the approach of many designers, who like to clump page elements like pix, main head and text in separate parts of the page or pair of pages. If the clustered pix leave the page looking unbalanced, a strong element – say text in heavy bold type – can be introduced opposite to compensate.

Biggest pic normally goes highest. There are plenty of exceptions. A story in a hamper [smaller item placed above the page lead] may be illustrated, with the main pic lower in the page. For variation a magazine may place the main pic and the headline on the bottom of the page. However, we need to have a reason for the biggest pic not to be the highest.

Cutout pix add momentum. Modular design, unless relieved, tends to be neat but lacking in life. One way to relieve this is for pix to be partly cut away from their rectangular borders. The top of a head edging out of the picture helps; more strikingly, background can be removed from the whole figure leaving text type to flow around the cutout shape.

OTHER VISUALS

This catch-all heading includes maps, charts, cartoons, drawings, fancy box rules, and pictures processed in special ways like producing a coarse-grained effect or removing all shades of grey so the pic is literally black and white. A range of visuals beyond photographs will make our layouts more effective.

Keep logos simple. Logos help identification of columns and other regular features, but they need to be right. Think of a favourite commercial logo, maybe the London Transport symbol or the rail station sign, and the chances are it will be very simple. The same should apply to editorial logos but often doesn't. They may be trying to say too much or, when they are made up on screen larger than lifesize, the artist may not have taken the effect of the reduction fully into account. Look at it actual size is a good rule.

Graphics give an added texture. Aside from their information value, maps and charts have a different visual texture from photographs and bring welcome variety to the page. The same is true of cartoons and drawings.

Choose specially processed photos. Not always, of course, but there are many other ways to run a photograph than straight. The issue, once again, is variety, particularly in the feature pages. Among the choices are coarsely screened pix, or bleached-out pix where only the blacks and the whites remain. Visually, these occupy a pleasing borderland between the realism of a photo and the interpretation of a drawing. Another possibility is to lay a light screen over the pic so it appears as seen through a veil.

SPACE

Don't be frightened of blank space. When space is precious, it is a natural journalistic impulse to fill every nook and cranny, but it's an impulse that must be overcome if pages are to be effective. Space normally means white space, yet the same considerations apply to magazine pages with coloured backgrounds. People who readily accept that a press release or a business letter is ruined by being overcrowded may find it impossible to leave part of a feature spread empty, the better to bring out the content. Hopefully, they will go the extra mile.

Uses of white space. A sense of the usefulness of white space runs through modern editorial design. We find it in increased spacing (leading) between lines of text, the choice to leave some lines of a headline short with the head set left to emphasise the white space, eyelines – a band running up the page or across the top that is left mainly empty – and above all blocks of the page, often next to the headline, left unoccupied. It takes self-confidence to leave a quarter of a pair of A4 pages blank in the name of design. Such confidence is unlikely to be misplaced. These are all examples of working white space.

ADVERTISEMENTS

Discover what the ad looks like. This may be easier said than done in some offices, but it's worth making the effort particularly on very important pages. The content of the ad may affect how we lay out our part of the page. We need to know at least whether the ad is mainly text, highly visual or with reversed-out lettering. A text ad gives us a free hand, but a pictorial ad will influence where or how we play our pictures. If the ad is a reverse-out, we would unbalance the page if we put a reverse headline nearby.

Where ads are placed. A single ad is placed on the outside of the page at the bottom. A second ad is either placed on top of the first ad, with subsequent ads stacking up the page, or placed at the opposite corner of the page, with subsequent ads placed alternately. The stacking system takes ads higher up the page and favours advertising. It may leave editorial little to work with at the top of the page. The opposite corner system, although it creates a potentially tricky bucket between the ads, leaves the top of the page open and favours editorial. It is undesirable to have both systems in use on the same publication because this sends out a confused visual signal. Filling in the bucket with a third ad, or placing a second ad beside the first ad rather than above it, are common placings but are not really fair to those advertisers, whose ads are relatively invisible.

Ensure ads are properly placed. The advertising department has the prerogative to place the ads, but we are entitled to find them placed according to an agreed system. If they aren't we should ask for them to be changed. The editor is responsible at law for the whole publication and officially has the last word.

19 Impact from Colour

COLOUR is abundant, colour is everywhere in media. Colour can be as much a jungle as a festival, and like any jungle we need guides to see us safely through. The typical printing process produces full colour – all the colours of the rainbow – from the three primary colours – blue [in printing terms, cyan], red [magenta] and yellow, with black to improve the faithfulness of the other colours. By the use of filters, the original picture is separated into the four colour values, and printing plates made accordingly. These plates in action successively build up the full-colour reproduction picture.

The use of spot colour is also common in newspapers and magazines. This is a single colour, involving no separation process, usually used for lettering rather than visuals. The internationally recognised Pantone system allows hundred of spot colours to be built up by mixing a range of core colours in appropriate proportions.

The colour wheel, illustrated below, is a handy guide to the choice of colours.

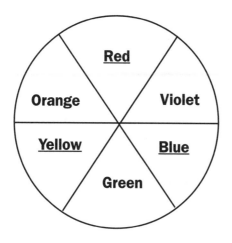

The colour wheel showing principal colours. Underlining shows the primary colours. Adjacent colours harmonise with each other. Opposite colours are contrasting

Prefer pix with strong colour content. This is the colour equivalent of choosing black and white pix with pronounced contrasts. A colour pic without a strong patch of colour will look washed out. It's not enough to say that content is paramount. The presence of colour adds another dimension that has to be taken into account. A possible solution for a pic that is strong in content but weak in colour is to run it as a duotone [a monochrome picture that is boosted by printing with a colour as well as black – see below].

Avoid one colour swamping the others in a full-colour pic. The most effective colour pix have two strong colours, or one strong colour with plenty of background colour variety. A picture that is taken over by various shades of a single colour – say a woman in a red dress in a room with red carpet and curtains – will be too strong and look unpleasant.

Use harmony colours for soft subjects. Yellow and orange are classic harmony colours, as are blue and green. Harmony colours are particularly appropriate for warm or happy subjects – fashion features or travel articles, for example. On the other hand, too much harmony can be soporific, so in a section seen as harmony colour it may be wise to inject some contrast colour too.

Use contrast colours for hard subjects. There is an obvious complementarity between contrasting, or hard, colours and hard subjects. We would normally expect news pix to be chosen for their contrasting colours. It is no accident that the two commonest colours for newspaper front page blurbs are red and blue – contrasting colours. Red and green are even more contrasting, but green is not as strong a colour as blue.

Black contrasts with everything. Including, curiously, colours like mauve and even dark blue. Fire scenes are among the most dramatic colour pix that a newspaper can use. Typically the fire is framed in areas of black and dark grey. As well as the strong contrast this gives, there is a second factor at work: colour may be the more effective for the scarcity of colour. This is a principle that advertisers know well. A dab of colour on a plain background makes the coloured object leap out.

Yellow and white don't go. It seems to be a rite of passage that every journalist and designer doing colour has to fall into this trap for himself or herself. Yellow does not show up well enough on white paper (unless the letters are outlined with black); white lettering out of a yellow background also will not show up properly. A common problem is coloured type overprinting a coloured pic with various parts of light and dark colours. A light colour like yellow shows up well against the dark parts but is lost against the light parts. (The same applies in reverse with dark lettering on a pic of mixed shades.)

Upbeat and downbeat. As well as harmonies and contrasts, we may need to consider another aspect of colour: Yellow is second only to white in luminosity. From there the luminosity scale is orange, red, green, blue, violet and black. The more luminous colours in a page, the more upbeat will be the feel. Where low-luminosity colours predominate, the feel of the page will be downbeat or low key. Yellow is popular as a background tint for text boxes. Because it is so luminous a very light screen, 10%-20%, should be used. Heavier screens are often used, producing a garish look.

Duotones lift black and white pix. A B&W picture will be swamped alongside a colour picture, and to preserve the balance of the page it needs to be enhanced. Duotoning is an effective technique in which the monochrome picture is printed in black and another colour, with the second printing screen angled differently. The effect is that the duotoned pic shows up more strongly alongside a colour pic. When well done, the pic may still look monochrome – until we compare it with a straight B&W when the difference becomes obvious. Another, less subtle way of enhancing a monochrome pic is to lay a light coloured screen over it.

Coloured type looks smaller. This is the opposite of what we might expect, but brightness is not to be confused with strength. Red is a bright, assertive colour, but put red text type next to the same size in black and it will look smaller. Dark blue will look closer to black, and may be an effective alternative, but its impact is partly because it has black in it. If coloured text type is to be used with black type, it needs to be larger or in bold.

Have a philosophy of colour use. How much colour, which colours and where are they to be used are all key design considerations. For headlines, boxes, tint backgrounds and page labels, the worst basis to choose a colour is simply that it's not the one we used on the previous page. Colour may mark out different sections of the publication. A colour may match the material: blue lettering to go with a feature on the Arctic is more appropriate than flaming orange. Or the headline colour may echo the dominant colour in the main picture, which neatly ties the two together.

20 Advertising Issues

ADVERTISEMENTS produce most of the income for most publications, with circulation usually a poor second. It is crucial for the commercial success of the enterprise. The demands of advertisers and the convictions of journalists often clash, however. Management has to try to resolve these tensions. There is little prospect of the editorial department being favoured at the expense of advertising, but there are many cases of the interests of advertising overriding those of editorial. While this produces short-term financial benefit, the product is bound to suffer in the long run.

Stick to deadlines for accepting ads. The last-minute acceptance of advertisements, beyond the official deadlines, is one of the biggest gripes of journalists. It means we don't know until the 11th hour and the 59th minute what space we have to work with. Even worse, existing material may have to be thrown out to make way for the late ad. The argument "It's all money" is very short-termist. If a strong but valid stance is taken on deadlines, advertisers will soon adapt to the earlier times.

Have maximum ad proportions on early pages. Every publication needs an agreed advertising: editorial ratio, with extra pages being triggered if advertisements accepted for a particular issue will put the proportion of ads over the limit. Beyond that, however, understandings are needed for the editorially crucial parts of the publication. Every advertiser wants to be on a righthand page, front of the book. But pages three and five, along with the front and back and in tabloids the centre spread, are the most important pages editorially. We want to have agreed limits to how much of those pages can be taken up with advertising. Paradoxically, the entire page sold as advertising is less damaging editorially than one that has, say, three-quarters advertising. Even so, we must hope that P3 isn't a whole-page ad too often! With magazines, where advertisements typically fill complete pages, the question is how much advertising is placed at the front of the book before significant chunks of editorial. The argument often heard that if advertisers aren't humoured they will go elsewhere is the philosophy of appeasing the playground bully – a damagingly limited strategy.

Label ad features. Advertising features, or advertorial, is text-based material that is trying to sell something. An advertiser books space and uses it for a promotional feature rather than a display ad. Or our advertising department creates an article on, say, Trends in Garden Equipment and around it sells ads from manufacturers and garden centres. Advertorial should be distinguished from editorial content – a line of smaller type above the headline saying Advertising feature or Advertisement feature is best – but sadly often the line isn't there.

Make special supplements look different. One of the murkiest areas of journalism for many years has been special supplements about countries, industries and so on. They are money-spinners either because the country or industry concerned has sponsored all the pages or because advertisers are rushing to be included. Special supplements are advertorials writ large. Articles are often of a high standard, and the national papers sometimes claim that the same editorial standards apply to these articles as to standard news and features. The claim is disingenuous, however, because as promotional material punches will have to be pulled somewhere along the line. For identification, the words Special supplement or Sponsored supplement can be included on the front page. At the least, different headline types should be used to mark the material out from editorial.

Make ads look different from editorial. There is a good case for using a different set of headline types for advertorials. The same can be said about display ads, but we can only control the ads composed in-house.

Many ads will be supplied by agencies as standard designs. Confusion of ads and editorial is particularly a problem with design-led magazines where fancy advertising displays and fancy editorial displays can look identical. It becomes difficult to know where one ends and the other begins.

Rule off ads from editorial. Ads need to be separated from editorial by light column rules (regardless of whether the style within the editorial section is to use rules or not). A rule box around the ad itself, a reverse block or any other solid feature is not enough to make the separation. Rules are not normally needed between the ads themselves since most ads are boxed, blocked or otherwise defined. Rules should be used, however, if an ad is so open that the text would run into the next ad.

Don't give an editorial mention in exchange for an ad. Enthusiastic sales reps often promise companies an editorial "mention" if they book an ad, and journalists feel they have to agree to do a story. On some newspapers and magazines the practice is institutionalised with an ad booking triggering an editorial writeup. Both practices are quite unacceptable because they amount to selling editorial space. This breaches the covenant with readers that material is included solely on its journalistic merit.

Don't charge/pay to use press releases. Press releases are sent out by organisations big and small in the hope that the media will find them newsworthy enough to use, or at least to treat as a tip to be followed up by the publication's own journalists. This activity has grown into a huge industry. A few publications have started to ask money from companies and PR agencies to print a press release as a news item. This may have developed from the practice of asking companies to pay for colour separations if a colour pic is to go with the material. This practice is itself deplorable (it is compromising the independence of the news columns to make willingness to pay a factor in inclusion), but it is nothing like as bad as charging to print news. This is simply corrupt. It is another form of selling the editorial space, even more damaging than editorial in support of advertising because there is no way for readers to see that money changed hands.

Company specialists are useful. PR people increasingly offer newspapers and magazines articles to run as editorial (not advertorial). Often these will be by specialists on the staffs of the companies the PR people represent. Provided that everyone plays by the rules, these articles are welcome. They offer something for all concerned: the expert gets a byline, the company gets a mention and the publication gets a usually well informed article free! The writer should not plug his or her company excessively or do competitors down. The publication should identify the writer as comercially or professionally involved in the subject under review.

Be positive about ads. And be careful, we could be replaced by a shopper [a publication entirely of ads]! Advertisements aren't just a nuisance, as some journalists see them. Not only do they pay our salaries or fees, but we even depend on ads for much of the editorial colour we enjoy. Without colour ads there would be far fewer pages available in colour. It is the demand for a colour advertisement that determines the presence of colour on many pages.

Index